My Role /

The Deacon's Role: From A Biblical Perspective

Copyright:
This book is the sole property of Dr. Joseph R. Rogers, Sr. and it is not to be copied or sold without written consent. (cc: 2010)

Dr. Joseph R. Rogers, Sr.

Dedication

As I write this second volume concentration on Leadership, I want to focus primarily upon the office of the Deacon-Servant.

I am grateful to the Lord for His insights and for giving me another opportunity to share with those who have been give the privilege and task to grace this office.

I dedicated it to you. Why? You Are Worthy!

First, that you will serve with unselfish honor, commitment, character and integrity.

Secondly, that you will ingest this wealth of knowledge and apply it as you serve the Lord's people.

Finally, that you will purchase unto yourself and good degree and be an asset to the church that you serve.

In closing, I commend you as you serve and I lift you up in prayer continually that you might be all that God has destined you to be.

As you serve as a **Deacon-Servant** will the Church Fellowship be enhanced because of you? Will the church fellowship develop and be all that God has destined it to be because of you?

These are **pertinent questions** that you must ask yourself and then do your best serving in office as a Deacon-Servant with the Holy Ghost leading you.

If you serve well, assisting the Pastor as the bible has so commanded—you will hear the welcome voice of The Master, Jesus Christ, say, **"Well Done Thou Good And Faithful Servant...etc"**.

Serve Well!

Joseph R. Rogers, Sr., D. Min.

Table Of Contents

                                    Page No

Dedication-------------------------- 2

Introduction------------------------ 6

I. The Problems The Church Faced----- 9

II. The Priorities The Church Faced-- 13

III. The Proposal The Church Faced--- 18

IV. The Rewards Of Selecting A Deacon- 26

V. The Requirements For A Deacon------ 33

VI. The Deacon And The Family--------- 44

VII. Closing Thoughts To The Deacon--- 51

VIII. The Discipline Of A Deacon------ 52

IX. A Journey Through History--------- 55

X. Tidbits To The Deacon-------------- 62

XI. The Deacon's Questionnaire-------- 65

	Page No
XII. The Author's Contact/Other Works-	73
XIII. Notes--------------------------	85

Introduction

There is much information available addressing the issue of the Deacon Ministry. While there is a wealth of information printed, the main thrust is whether or not it is relevant and in line with the Bible.

Most of the information that I have read and researched conveys or address the Deacon's Ministry from a denominational and secular perspective, rather than a biblical one.

While some of the information sounds good; that alone is not good enough; it must be bible based. No one should be allowed to serve in this office solely because they are good persons in the community, pay a lot of money in the offering or hold a high position in the secular setting.

The bible is clear and precise when it comes to selecting persons to serve as deacons (servants).

- **Salvation** is a must.
- **Wisdom** is a must.

- **Being Filled** with Holy Spirit is a must.

The local church must not allow any person to serve in this important Leadership role who is **not qualified**.

I hope to shed some light on this issue of selecting Deacons to serve by seeing what the bible says about the subject.

Why? Because the final authority for all matters of faith and practices in the body of Christ is the Word of God.

Therefore, we are not going to concern ourselves with what men have to say about the Deacon Ministry Role in the church. We're going to stick with what the Bible commands.

The bible is clear as to "why" deacons were selected to serve and the succeeding qualifications which are to be followed, when selecting these people.

The Apostle Paul in his letter to his son in the ministry Timothy, (1 Timothy 3) and Dr. Luke, in The Acts Of The Apostles (Acts 6) share that information with us.

We can also look in the Old Testament writing of Moses (Deuteronomy 1). Let us make it clear that the "Local Church" was formed and was duly operating without the office of the deacon.

I am in no way trying the **discredit the office**—it's biblical and it's needed! The Deacons (Servants) can be blessings to the Pastor and Church when those who serve understand and execute what their roles entail.

Lastly, be reminded that Leadership was not the problem when selecting Deacons-Servant. The problem was **selecting helpers to assist the Apostles (Pastors).**

Joseph R. Rogers, Sr., D. Min.
Servant/Pastor/Teacher

I. THE -PROBLEMS- THE CHURCH FACED: (v. 1)

Let us begin by looking at what really was the situation that the Church faced. Again, I say very authoritatively, **it was not the lack of unqualified leadership.** Observe the Scripture below...

Acts 6:1-*"And in those days, when the number of the disciples was multiplied, there arose a murmuring (complaining) of the Grecians against the Hebrews, because their <u>widows were neglected in the daily ministration</u>"*.

What an insight! Verse one exposes a conflict that was brewing in the early church. People were not being ministered to. Not because of purposeful neglect, but because of an explosion in growth.

When trouble comes into the church, it must be faced head-on and dealt with, and not allowed to simmer and brew. This problem was no one persons fault—it was growth!

    A. <u>The Problem Of -Multiplication-</u>:
Three thousand (3,000) people were saved at Pentecost; another Five thousand

(5,000) were saved shortly thereafter, excluding women and children.

It is estimated that the church in Jerusalem numbered between 20,000 and 50,000 at this time. As a church grows larger so does its potential for problems (ministering to all of the people).

As a church grows larger so does its need for good strong godly leadership. According to the bible, this new found New Testament Christian was growing by leaps and bounds.

B.   The Problem Of -Murmuring-:
There were two classes of people in the early church. There were the **Aramaic speaking** Jews who were native to Israel, and there were the **Greek speaking,** Hellenistic Jews.

The Bible tells us that they were **"murmuring"**. This word refers to **"secret debate; whispering"**. People were talking about others in a negative manner. When needs of the peoples goes lacking, the Devil tries to explode the situation into something larger than what it really is.

The same is still holds true today! If the devil cannot infiltrate us and attack us from without, you can rest assured he (Satan) will try to do it from within. He will do everything he can to divide us and cause us to attack one another.

As in the fellowship then and certainly in the fellowship today there need to be an atmosphere conducive for **worship, praise, growth, development, peace and harmony. Murmuring** is never the answer!

As a matter of fact, God was angered when some of the Israelites for murmured against their Leaders, **Moses and Aaron.** The local assembly is no place for **anger, un-forgiveness, division, strife, dissention,** and **back-biting.** The House of the Lord is the **"House of Prayer For All People".**

  C. <u>The Problem Of -Ministry-</u>:
The Greek speaking widows were not getting their share of the daily food supply. Evidently, the Apostles were responsible for seeing to it that the people, especially the widows had the **food** and other essentials needs.

  As the church grew, the task became too large for the Apostles and some people were inevitably missed in the daily food allotments.

The church today still faces similar problems. In our day the burden of ministry in the church, in most cases, has been placed on the shoulders of the Pastor, simply, because he is paid a salary.

In a small church this is a challenging task. In a larger church it is absolutely impossible! When everything rest on the shoulders of the Pastor, some people are going to be neglected and they are going to be offended.

It is humanly impossible for the Pastor alone to do everything that is needed to have a wholesome church.

II. THE -PRIORITIES- THE CHURCH FACED: (v. 2)

Acts 6:2-"Then the twelve called the multitude of the disciples unto them, and said, it is not reason that we should leave the word of God, and serve tables".

When this conflict arose, the Apostles took charge of the situation. They were trying to be everywhere and do everything.

Shortly into the process they found it to be an impossible task. They reminded the people of the **priorities of ministry** (preaching & teaching). We need to be reminded of those priorities today as well.

A. The Priority Of Preaching:
Acts 6:2b- "...It is not reason that we should leave the word of God, and serve tables.

RVS says, "It does not make sense for us to put off the necessary preparation for the preaching ministry of the church and wait on tables."

The Apostles recognized that their primary responsibility was preparation for the ministry of the Word. This involved three elements: **prayer, preparation and preaching.** The bible says, "But we will give ourselves continually to prayer and to the ministry of the word". (6:4).

These Preachers (Apostles) were not called and anointed of God to hand out groceries. They were not called to deal with every little issue that arose in the conger-gation. They were called to 'teach' and 'preach' the Word of God.

Handing out groceries and attending to every little minor situation would take way from the time that they needed for pray and prepare for the preaching and teaching service.

Nothing in this church or in any other church will ever be more important than the time when the pastor walks to this pulpit, opens his Bible and begins to preach. Nothing equals that!

Remember:

- o If the preaching is to have power,

- If the worship service is to have anointing,
- If people lives are to be impacted,
- If the Devil is to be horrifies,
- If God is to be glorified…

The Pastors must have time quality time to prepare properly! For the preacher, preparation is the number one priority!

B. The Priority Of People:
Sermons are important, but having some one to preaching to (people) is a priority too! It is important to understand that people are the main focus of ministry, whether they are being ministered to in word, deeds or needs.

The salvation of the souls of men was Jesus' main reason for coming to planet earth (redemption).

In that, the world and the church is made up of people there is going to be a need for ministry, both physically and spiritually.

Now I am aware of the fact that there are Pastors who have the drive and will to be helpful and hands on; but one must think realistically and understanding that everyone is human and most of all they are limited.

It was impossible for the Apostles then to efficiently handle the task and it is impossible for the Pastors today to do it all by themselves.

This is why Deacons (Servants) were selected and or appointed to **'handles this business'**. **'This business'** is not lording over the church, **'this business'** is assisting the pastor as he/she minister to the people needs.

- ✓ The Pastor can visit, but he cannot visit everyone.

- ✓ The Pastor can go to the hospital, but he cannot spend his whole day there.

- ✓ The Pastor can be available, but not all the time.

There are times when Pastor must shut in and tarry with the Lord, with the Bible in order to get a Word from Heaven for the people.

Beloved, it comes down to a matter of priorities! The Deacon must be available to **'help' or 'assist'** the Pastor when it comes to meeting the needs of the congregation.

III. THE -PROPOSAL- THE CHURCH FACED: (v. 3-5)

Acts 6:3-5-"Wherefore, brethren, look ye out among you seven men of honest report, full of the Holy Ghost and wisdom, whom we (the apostles) may appoint over this business".

Doing the setting of this text there were too many needs and not enough people to meet those needs.

The Apostles ask the people (church family) to recommend (select) seven (7) people to help or assist them in handling this situation (the daily administration).

Let's dissect these verses and see what the office of a Deacon is all about.

A.   They Faced A -Selection-:
The church was told to choose from among themselves "seven men…whom we (the apostles) may appoint over this business".

Even though the church membership had the privilege of selecting someone, they were mindful of the fact that the selected person(s) must by approved by the Apostles (Pastors).

Now the phrase "**over this business**" has been taken out of context and misunderstood for years. The Deacons were not selected to be the **church or pastor bosses.**

The Church Family did not have a problem with lack of leadership. What the church needed were assistants (servants) to help the Leaders (Pastors) ministry to the local assembly.

The Deacons are not over the "business" of the church. The Deacons were/are selected to assist the Pastors in ministering to the widows/tables of the local assembly.

And whatever else the pastor or church is in need of to keep the fellowship moving along smoothly. There is no scripture that directly or indirectly implies that Deacon(s) runs a church family.

The Deacons serve at the pleasure of the Pastor and the Church! Deacons are to be committed and faithful to the position as church disciples first and then servants.

In some churches the 'deacon(s)' is/are appointed for life. In some churches the 'deacon(s)' are selected on the term basis i.e., (2, 3, 4 years). Each church must choose which model fits their local fellowship.

However, keep in mind that there are qualifications to be followed when selecting a deacon and these qualifications cannot be thrown away after a deacon is ordained.

Any Deacon can be <u>removed</u> (set down or removed) from his office by the Pastor and Church at any time. Deacons are servants, not rulers! Deacons are appointed and without question, they can be <u>disappointed</u>!

Should there be Deacon Chairman? What are their duties? All the models that I have researched in the bible I have found that none of them indicate that there is a need for a Deacon Chairman!

In my opinion all a "Chairman" ends up being is a **"Little Pastor"**, therefore creating even a larger problem. Why? A Church can have only one Pastor. Anything with two heads is called, **"A Monster"**.

Now, it may be expedient that you select a Chairman, but keep in mind its potentials. In my opinion, if there is to be a Chairman, it should be the Pastor of the Church.

Now, the "business" they were placed over was the "business" of "serving tables", (v. 2).

Thus, a Deacon is a person who is chosen to be a servant of/to the church. Any Deacon who sees the office of a Deacon as a position of power does not deserve to be selected for the office.

It is important that the Deacon be a **"tither"** and **"attends"** all church services, especially the teaching services (bible study) of the Pastor. How can the Deacon get the heart of the Pastor and the vision of the church if they are absent from the main services of the church?

B. They Faced A -Challenge-:
While the people were told to choose servants, they were to make sure that these persons be of a **special character, integrity and quality.**

For Biblical understanding we will consider the three qualifications mentioned in these verses. The candidates were to have three special characteristics.

1. Deacons Are To Be People of Integrity:
"of honest report".
This phrase refers to people who "have experienced something." It speaks of people who by their testimony and lifestyle have earned the love and respect of the church.

2. Deacons Are To Be Spiritual People:
"full of the Holy Ghost". This means that they are to be Spirit-filled and Spirit-controlled.

The Deacons are to be people, who are in tune with God; led by God and who display godly ways in their lives (Galatians 5:22-23).

The church will forever 'regret' selecting people who are not full of the Holy Ghost. A person who is not filled with the Spirit will become a **'thorn'** in the side of the church.

3. **Deacon Are To Be Gifted People: "full of...wisdom".** This means they are to be able to make sensible decisions. They are to be people who listen to others, but after listening to others, not be influenced by negative **selfish personal motives.**

In other words, there is to be no **buddy system** and **favoritism** when it comes to ministering to God's people.

Deacons are to make their decisions based on what **"thus saith the Lord".** They must be people who can move beyond their own boundaries (wants, selfishness) to see the needs of others.

> ❖ The Church needs people who are godly and gifted.

> ❖ The Church does not need people who are just business minded and not Spirit led.

- ❖ The Church does not need people who have a lot of money and but no Wisdom.

- ❖ The Church do not need people who are a certain age, but people who knows God; knows His voice and who have a heart to serve.

C. <u>They Faced A -Choice</u>-:
The church got together and made their selections. These people were presented to the Apostles for final approval.

If the Pastor rejects someone who has been selected from the congregation the Pastor's judgment must respected.

God will **chastise (admonish)** the Pastor who lay hands on a person who is not qualified to serve as a Deacon, regardless of how other Church members feel.

Remember, the text said, *"That we (The Pastor) may appoint over this business"*.

If people of God follow the plan of God the church will prosper. The early church chose the right people and benefited from it. If we choose the right people, we will benefit as well.

    The Church needs people who will take up their assigned mantel of service and execute their duties.
    The Church needs people who are godly and gifted to meet the needs of the church.

    The Church does not need people who want power, prestige and position.

    The Church does not need people who are just looking for titles and offices.

    The Church needs **SERVANTS OF GOD WHO ARE WILLING TO SERVE THE PEOPLE OF GOD!**

    The right choice **insures** growth and blessings.
    The wrong choice **hinders** the things of God.

    Choosing Deacons is a very serious and should never be based upon personal friendship, secular position or favoritism—**it must be strictly biblical based!**

IV. THE -REWARDS- OF SELECTING THE DEACON:
(Acts 6:7; 1 Timothy 3:13)

Acts 6:7-"And the word of God increased; and the number of the disciples multiplied in Jerusalem greatly; and a great company of the priests were obedient to the faith".

A. THE REWARDS TO THE CANDIDATE:
1 Timothy 3:13-"For they that have used the office of a deacon well purchase to themselves a good degree, and great boldness in the faith which is in Christ Jesus".

When people serve as Deacons and serves well, they will receive **spiritual rewards** from the Lord and thank you very much from the local church.

a. Spiritual Promotion:
"purchase to themselves a good degree"

This phrase means "they obtain for themselves an excellent rank." The word "degree" means "rank or standing".

The Deacon who serves the church, in the manner consistent with the teachings of the Word of God, will be exalted.

Not only will the church promote a faithful Deacon, God Himself will honor the person who faithfully serves others.

James 4:10-"Humble yourselves in the sight of the Lord, and he shall lift you up".

1 Peter 5:6-"Humble yourselves therefore under the mighty hand of God, that he may exalt you in due time".

The Deacon who possesses **godly character** and **integrity** will serve the church well because they are humble in the Lord and they do not seek after the **praises of men.**

The godly Deacon will serve the church well because they have a heart for the glory of God and a desire to see their church grow and prosper.

b. **Spiritual Power:**
"great boldness in the faith"

As the Deacons serve the Lord and the church they will see the Lord use them in a mighty and special way.

In doing so, their faith in the Lord will be strengthened and their walk with the Lord will grow deeper and stronger.

Stephen and Phillip are two good examples to every Deacon. If you are serving as a "Deacon" or have been selected to serve, let me encourage you to know that you serve the Lord by serving others and your rewards will be great.

B. THE REWARDS TO THE CHURCH:
Acts 6:7b-" ...and the number of the disciples multiplied in Jerusalem greatly:"

Not only do the Deacons, themselves, reap certain benefits, so does the church. In fact, the church is the greatest recipient when they have committed godly Deacons serving.

Now let me show you a few of the ways the church benefits from Deacons serving well.

a. In The Arena Of -Peace-:
The Deacons were selected because there was division in the church. Some of the widows felt left out when the daily food rations.

The contentions between the two groups were growing so much that it could have potentially caused them to split.

However, because of the discernment of the Apostles, **assistants** (servants, deacon) were selected to carry out the work of serving tables in the church. This decision pleased both sides.

Some people aren't going to be happy no matter what you do. That is just the way things are. You cannot and will not please all the people all the time.

Godly, serving Deacons helps the Pastor and Church achieve the goal of ministering to the people. There is nothing more rewarding that seeing your church **unified**.

b. In The Arena Of -Provision-:
Because the Apostles were so busy preaching, praying and teaching the widows in the church were not getting their needs met.

But, after Deacons were **selected and appointed** the needs of the widows were taken care of.

When the Pastor and Deacons are serving as they should, the sick and shut-ins are ministered to; the needs of the church are taken care of and the burdens and concerns of the church are handled in an effective manner.

c. In The Arena Of Preaching:

When the Deacons were selected, the Apostles had the time they needed to pray and study and prepare for ministry.

Because, they could pray and study as they should, the ministry of the Word of God spread in the church and community.

The church benefited because the preaching got more powerful. As the preaching improved, the people were fed a full course meal and the church grew spiritually and physically.

d. In The Arena Of People:

The people could do nothing but rise to the next level. Their thirsty for more Word increased and when that happens, people participate more.

They will become more developed and this will in turns equip them to be better witnesses. When the body is function properly the church will be greatly expanded.

When the responsibility of the total church operation does not rest solely upon the Pastor the church will grow and prosper—this was/is why Deacons were/are selected to serve.

C. <u>THE REWARDS TO THE COMMUNITY</u>:
Acts 6:7c-" …and a great company of the priests were obedient to the faith.

We have seen that the 'Deacons' will be rewarded for their faithful service to the church.

We have seen that the **'Church'** will be rewarded as their needs are addressed and met by leaders.

Now, let us see how the Community will also benefit from the Church having the right kind of Deacons.

a. Sinners Will Be Converted:
A "great multitude" came into the church because the Gospel was proclaimed in more power and more clarity. Many people were reached and a tremendous number of people came to Jesus for salvation.

The Church will grow when things are in line with and done according to God's Word. When the Pastor has time to study and prepare in delivering the Word; the Holy Spirit will convict the sinner to repentance.

When the Pastors are free to do their jobs, the church will grow; the community will grow.

The above are the "Rewards" that come when God's will was/is honored in the selection of Deacons-Servants.

Thank God For Godly Deacons!

V. THE REQUIREMENTS OF THE DEACON:

We have learned that the office of Deacon was created to fill a void in the church.

We learned that the Deacons were never intended to function as "church or pastor bosses".

We have learned that Deacons are to be the servants of God to the people, looking after their needs as directed by the Pastors.

We have learned that the word "Deacon" translates a word that means "a table waiter; a domestic servant; one who attends to the needs of others."

Now that we have a clearer understanding of what role the Deacon plays in the church, let's turn our attention to the **"qualifications"** for the office.

The Bible is crystal clear concerning the kind of person that is to be considered for the office of Deacon.

A. THE DEACON AND FAITH:
Any person who serves as a Deacon in the Christian Church must be a person of faith. Their faith should be evident in **their words, their works and their walk.**

    a. The Deacon Must Be A Saved Person:
In Acts 6:3 the church was told to "look ye out among you seven men..." In other words, the Deacons were to be active members of the community of faith (the Church). The phrase implies that they were/are to be saved people.

While only God knows the condition of any person's heart; there is certain evidence that will help the pastor's and churches see where another person stands with the Lord.

For your consideration:

1. Do they have a clear testimony of a life changing salvation experience? (St. John 3:3)

2. Do they live a clean, holy life? (2 Corinthians). 5:17.

3. Is the Lord, their faith and their church a major part of their life? (Hebrews 11:6)

4. Do they walk in love toward the brethren? Are that they examples to their families. (1 John 3:14-15)

While none of us are in a position to judge the salvation experience of other person, the Lord Jesus Christ did say that a person's **spiritual root** would be proven by their **spiritual fruit**, (St. Matthew 12:33).

Our **"fruit inspection"** is in order. When we are considering people for Deacons, we must be sure that we're selecting saved persons who are full of the Holy Ghost and Wisdom.

b. The Deacon Must Be A Separated Person:
In Acts 6:3 it says-"of honest report" - This phrase means that the people chosen to be Deacons must have a good name among the people within the Church Family and in the community. The Deacons must be people of personal integrity.

***They must be people who will do the right thing regardless of the personal cost.

***They must be people who speak the truth in their words and in their walk.

***They must be blameless, which is to say they must be people to whom no one can point an accusing finger against and bring charges that are true.

***They must be people who live for Jesus at home, on the job, in the community and in the church.

***They must be people who are worthy of the respect of the church family.

c. The Deacon Must Be A Spiritual Person:
Again, in Acts 6:3 the bible says— "full of the Holy Ghost" – The Deacons are to be people controlled and led by the Spirit of God.

The command found in Ephesians 5:18 must be true in the Deacon's life. The word "full" means, "thoroughly permeated with; complete; lacking nothing, perfect."

Deacons are to demonstrate that they are Spirit-filled by constantly displaying the "fruit of the Spirit", (Galatians 5:22-23)

d. The Deacon Must Be A Sensible Person:
Again in Acts 6:3 it says, "full of wisdom" - These word does not imply that the Deacons must be college educated men with a lot of degrees.

It does mean that they are to be people who can make sensible decisions based on the Word of God.

A person of wisdom does not allow his judgment to be clouded by emotion, personal opinion, family or peer pressure, or any other external influences.

A person of wisdom listens for the voice of God and does what the Lord leads them to do.

e. The Deacon Must Be A Scriptural Person:
In 1 Timothy 3:9, it says- "holding the mystery of the faith in a pure conscience". The emphasis of this verse

is that Deacons are to be people who know the doctrines of the faith and who live them out in their lives consistently.

"Holding the mystery of the faith" speaks of the entire New Testament truth.

"In a pure conscience" has the idea that the Deacons are to be people who not only know the truth, but who live out that truth in their daily lives. The Deacons must not and should not talk one way and live another!

A person who is to be a Deacon must be student of the bible. The Deacons must know **"what"** they believe; **"why"** they believe it and they must **"live out"** that same belief (faith).

B. THE DEACON AND FAITHFULNESS:
The personal faith of the Deacon is vitally important. When this happens, the Deacon will exhibit certain characteristics.

a. The Deacon Will Be Faithful In Temperament:
The Deacon is to be <u>**"grave"**</u> (serious). This word does not mean that a Deacon should never smile or have a sense of humor.

By the same token, a Deacon must not be a flippant (jokey) or a silly person who makes light of serious spiritual matters.

Deacons should enjoy life and be joyous and happy, but should also understand that some things are serious and should be treated with the respect.

The word "grave" means "honorable, worthy of respect, pious and holy". It refers to a person who is held in high esteem for the godly lifestyle they lead.

b. The Deacon Will Be Faithful In Speech:
The bible says, **"not double-tongued"** - This word literally means a person talks out of both sides of his mouth.

The Deacon must be a person who is in control of his tongue. A loose tongue is clear evidence that a person is not filled with the Spirit.

James 1:26-"If any man (person) among you seems to be religious, and bridleth not his tongue, but deceiveth his own heart, this man's religion is vain".

Now, let us look at this matter of the tongue from a three-fold perspective.

1. The Deacon must not be the kind of person who will say one thing to one person and another thing to someone else.

2. The Deacon must not be a gossiper. The Deacon is not to slander of others and use their positions to sling dirt.

3. The Deacon must be a person whose 'word' is dependable; that is, you can count on it. The Deacon should not be a person who is careless with the truth.

 c. **The Deacon Will Be Temperant: (In Control)**
The bible says, **"Not given to much wine"**. This means a person that should not be given to drunkenness or other forms of substance abuse.

The Deacon must be a person under the control of the Spirit and not other mind altering chemicals.

The Deacon must be a person that "abstains from all appearance of evil".

The key word is **abstain** means to **refrain, withdraw, give up.**

    d. The Deacon Will Be In Control All Of Temptations: (Money)
The bible says <u>"**Not greedy of filthy lucre**"</u> - This phrase literally means "not out to make a dishonest dollar". And, definitely a person who have their own finance in control.

This also related to all other things (opposite sex, power, position...etc.) which can cause the Deacon to lose focus on what they should be doing.

    e. The Deacon Will Be Able To Withstand Testing:
The Bible says, <u>"**let these also first be proven**"</u>. The word "proven" means "to test, to examine, and to scrutinize".

It is a must that the Deacon be mature enough to handle people, problems and situations that arises, in a professional way. The Deacons cannot loose it (blow up, exhibit anger in the public)

This suggests, I believe, that a new Christian should not be chosen as a Deacon. Why?

Because a new Christian has not had time to mature, develop and demonstrate the need kind of testimony that is required.

Because, a new Christian have not had the time to grow in the faith.

Because a new Christian has not had time to show that they are made out of the real stuff.

    c. **The Deacon Will Be Faithful In Testimony: "Lifestyle".**
The bible says, **"blameless"** – This word has the idea of **"being above reproach"**. It literally means "one who cannot be arraigned or brought up on charges."

The Deacon should be like **Teflon**. Which is to say, when charges are made, there will not be enough evidence for them to stick.

The Deacon personal life, public life, family life and faith life must be **impeccable.**

42

f. **The Deacon Will Be Faithful In Tasks:<u>"let them use the office of a Deacon"</u>.**
The bible says, <u>**"use" and not "fill"**</u>. There are too many persons who want to **"fill"** (for power, prestige, recognition) this office and too few who are willing to **"use"** (for ministry, helping) this office.

How does a Deacon **"use"** the office of Deacon? The Deacon uses this office by actively displaying a servant's attitude in:

1. Visiting The Sick, Hurting, Grieving.
2. Supporting The Vision of The Church.
3. Helping The Pastor.
4. Work With Other Church Disciples
5. Doing Any Other Assigned Tasks.
6. Paying Tithes & Offerings
7. Being Present At All Church Services.

VI. THE DEACON AND THE FAMILY:

Another area of the Deacon's life that needs to be considered is the area of the Deacon's family life.

First, God has certain standards that He expects the Deacons to maintain in their homes. Any person who does not maintain these standards are not qualified to serve.

Second, some people believe that the Deacon must be married. The Bible does not directly say that single persons are disqualified. The bible just talks about the married. Because of this one can assume that single persons are not qualified.

The bible does say, <u>"Let the Deacon be the husband of one wife"</u>.

The bible does say, <u>"Having their children under subjection"</u>.

Does this eliminate a single person? Well, in principle it may, but philosophically it does not. It simply gives guidelines for those who are married and who do have children.

I believe that single person can be appointed to serve as a Deacon. However, if they should marry and have children, the Lord does expect them adhere to the rules.

A. A Word About The Deacon's Marriage:"Let the Deacons be the husbands of one wife..."
There are various interpretations of this phrase. There are those who say that it means the Deacons can have only **"one spouse at a time."** That is to say, a person can be divorced, remarry and still serve.

There are those who say it means the Deacon is to be "a one woman man". That is to say, a divorced person cannot serve if they married and their previous spouse is still living.

I would suggest to you that you follow the Scriptures and let the chips fall as they may.

The Deacons as the Pastors are examples to the church and held in high standards and should be living above reproach in their spiritual life as well as their married life.

I would also suggest that the Leadership of the Church **adopt a rule to follow and stick with it.**

(The agreement is simply this: We agree that a **single person** and married person who have been divorced and remarry can serve as deacons in this church).

To try to unweave this web will take more time than I have and in doing so it would only be **opinionated in nature.** I just know what the bible says.

B. <u>A Word About The Deacon' Management</u>: "<u>ruling their children and their own houses well</u>".
The Deacons must be in control of their homes. The Deacon's spouse and children should respect them in the home.

If Deacons cannot gain the respect of their immediate family they will probably not gain the respect of their church family.

The Deacons should be persons who are in control of their wealth (money), possessions (things that they have accumulated) and their behavior and the behavior (action) of their family.

Remember, Deacons as well as Pastors are to be examples to the church. Their homes (spouse & children) should be the models of what a Christian home should be.

Now, granted the Deacon cannot control their family member against their will, but they should live in such a way that their family members will respect, listen to and follow their judgment.

    C. **A Word About The Deacon's Spouse:**
Many commentators, preachers as well as Christians look at this passage to be referencing the serving Deacon's spouses.

What is a Deacon's spouse? It is the spouse of a Deacon or a female deacon. This is has been a debatable issue of the years. That is, should women be selected to serve in the office of the deacon?

I encourage each local fellowship to decide whether or not they are going to ordain women as "Deacons-Servant" and stick with their conviction.

I only ask you to keep in mind all of the bible scriptures and not just one scripture. It should be noted that God use both males and females.

    a. Debroah-------Judges 4:4-9
    b. Ester---------Esther 2:18
    c. Ruth----------Ruth 2:14
    d. Phebe---------Romans 16:1-2
    e. Priscilla-----Acts 18:1-3

Now, let us look at the requirements or qualifications as outlined in the Scriptures.

1. The Spouse's Temperament: "grave".

This word means "honorable, worthy of respect, pious and holy". Like the Deacon's, their spouses are to have lifestyles that are worthy of respect and held in high esteem in the church and at home.

Any Deacon's spouse who portrays foolishness, sinfulness and makes light of serious spiritual matters will be problematic. Like the Deacons, their spouse should live lives that are worth imitating.

2. **The Spouse's Tongue: "not slanderers".**
This means that the Deacon's spouses are to be person who can control their tongues. If the candidates spouse is a gossiper, slander, this should elimination the person from serving as Deacon.

3. **The Spouse Temperance: "sober". "Not a drunk" "out of control"**
The spouses of Deacons are to be free from addiction to chemicals. This word speaks of "abstaining from the immoderate use of wine".

A person who is married to a spouse who is under the control of chemical substances is not qualified to be a Deacon.

A person who is married to a spouse who is unable to control their temper, action or words is not qualified to a Deacon.

4. **The Spouse Trustworthiness: "faithful in all things".**
A Deacon's spouse is to be "absolutely trustworthy". Why is this important? Well, there will be some

delicate information that will come to the ears of the Deacon's spouse.

The Deacon's spouses must know how to guard personal and delicate information. If the Deacon's spouses are dependable, committed, and trustworthy they will be an asset to the Church.

The Deacon's spouse should not be a hindrance to their spouses nor the church fellowship.

VII. Closing Thoughts:

I know that these qualifications are "**rigid**", "**challenging**" and "**stiff**". They are intended to be! The office of the Deacon is a high and holy office.

A Deacon can either build up or tear down the reputation of the church by how they live their lives and execute their duties as a Deacon.

The Pastor and Church are only fooling themselves if they select just anybody to serve as a Deacon.

Selecting and Ordaining Deacons is the most serious thing a church ever does, outside of calling a Pastor.

If you follow the bible and do it right the church will be blessed in a mighty way.

If you follow your feelings and get it wrong, your church will pay for it for many years to come.

VIII. The Discipline Of The Deacon: (Should Deacons Be Removed?)

Most Pastors and Church fellowships have avoided dealing with this issue fearing it would split their church family.

The Deacons are selected to be helpers (servants) to the church and not a hindrance to it. There is no Deacon that cannot be replaced. The Deacons are **'appointed'** (selected to serve) and the Deacon can be **'disappointed'** (removed from office).

I would suggest that Churches follow the principles of the bible and set up some detailed guidelines as it relates to selecting deacons, deacons serving and deacons remaining as servants.

When one is asked to serve in the office of a Deacon; is it for life? **(until death)**! I would suggest that you take a hard look at this.

If a Pastor is found guilty of some infraction the church usually removed them. The same/similar principles should apply to the Deacon.

In all fairness, I would suggest that the Pastor and Church Family removed the Deacon in a professional way—that is, be Christian about it!

I believe and hope that you would agree that a Church Fellowship cannot allow a person to continue to 'serve' as a Deacon who is not willing to follow the prescribed bible guidelines.

The Apostle Paul writing to the Thessalonians for the second time said this:

2 Thessalonians 3:6-"Now we command you, brethren, in the name of our Lord Jesus Christ, that ye withdraw yourselves from every brother that walketh disorderly, and not after the tradition (bible principles, truths) which he received of us.

2 Thessalonians 3:7-"For yourselves know how ye ought to follow us: for we behaved not ourselves disorderly among you;

In the local fellowship there must be rules and has guidelines to be adhered to. If this does not happen, the Church Family will soon find itself operating in disorder, which leads to chaos, which eventually ends up in destruction.

The office of Deacon is very important. All deacons are not a thorn in the church's side and enemies to the Pastor.

This Ministry (Deacons, Servants) frees up the Pastor to do preaching and teaching; which therefore allowing the Church Family to develop and mature in the word of God.

Serve Well!
Joseph R. Rogers, Sr., D. Min

IX. A Journey Through History:

In all of my research surrounding this very important topic, I have found many views and opinions as it relates to the duties and responsibilities of the Pastor and the Deacon.

At the conception of the local church fellowship (Pentecost (Acts 1, 2) one must admit that the Church was formed without the ministry of deacons.

Now, this is in no way saying that the Ministry of the deacons is not needed. To the contrary, one must admit that there is a need for this office.

Any position that has been sanctioned by God is in order. The problem comes when people who **serve** in this offices, become **power drunk** and **selfish**.

The calling out or selecting helps or assistant to handle some of the day to day responsibilities came into being doing the time of The Nation of Israel journeyed from Egypt to the Promised Land.

As the Hebrew Nation grew the task for *Moses* became too much of a burden. Therefore, he was instructed by his father-in-law, **Jethro** to summons some helpers to handle the day to day situation (Deuteronomy Chapter One).

Moses asked the people to choose **captains** to handle the needs, problems and other situations that arose within the congregation's day to day operating.

A. The Selections, Problems & Solutions:
Deuteronomy 1:9-"And I spake unto you at that time, saying, I am not able to **bear** you myself alone: [10] The LORD your God hath **multiplied you**, and, behold, ye are this day as the stars of heaven for multitude.

Deuteronomy 1:12-" How can I myself alone bear your cumbrance, and your burden, and your strife"?

Deuteronomy 1:13-"Take you wise men, and understanding, and known among your tribes, and I (Moses) will make them rulers over you.

If you will notice the problem was ministering to the people. The Leader, Moses did not have time to do it all. Assistants (servants) were then selected to help in the process.

The New Testament calling of servants follows the **same pattern** as the Old Testament. The Leaders did not have the time to take care of the day to day tasks.
 (NT references, Acts 6:1-6).

The Assistants in the Old Covenant (NT, Deacons) were given instructions to follow when dealing the congregational issues that arose:

Deuteronomy 1:17-"Ye shall not respect persons in judgment; but ye shall hear the small as well as the great; ye shall not be afraid of the face of man; for the judgment is God's: and the cause that is too hard for you, bring it unto me, and I will hear it".

Since that time (Moses Time) and after the forming of the New Testament Church (Christian Church), Satan was and still is **aggravating** the local church causing strive, envy and fractions.

As we now look at what is called, **"A Historical Point Of View"**; tradition has confirmed that **"The Deacon Boards"**, rose to power because in many of our churches, Pastors were more like circuit preachers.

Which is to say; the Pastors only visited the Churches about **one of twice in a month**. Therefore, the control or influence of leadership in the church was given to the **board of deacons** by the local congregation.

It has been documented also that this power struggle (deacon board & Pastor) came about because of or the result of the type government that exist in most churches **(democratic-the majority rules)**.

I know that we live in a nation (US) that is **democratic** in government and it's good, but I belief the Church of God's government is a **"Theocracy"**, (a government by a God), rather than a **"Democracy" (a government of majority rule)**.

It is my conviction that God speaks to His people through His leaders (That's the bible Model). In a Democracy the people lead themselves.

During the time of the **Prophet Jeremiah** the Lord says this:

Jeremiah 23:4-"And I (God) will set up shepherds over them which shall feed them: and they shall fear no more, nor be dismayed, neither shall they be lacking, saith the LORD".

If God calls, anoints and sets the Leader in the Church. That same God uses those same leaders to delivers unto the people what He wants them to know.

The Pastor is **'called'** and **'anointed'** to lead the people in the things of God.

The Deacon is **'selected'** and **'appointed'** to assist the Pastor in carrying out the vision for that Church.

It grieves my heart when I see, Deacons and Pastors and even some church members fighting over the power (who is the boss).

I know that there are some Pastors who have their heads in the air.

I know that there are some Pastors who go about things as dictators.

In spite of this, that does not give a church or a person the right to do the wrong thing, just because someone else is doing wrong. If the **Pastor** is wrong, God will fix it.

My brothers and sisters do not destroy the local church body trying to get back at some person.

My brothers and sister do not throw the baby out with the bath water.

So, where are we now? Well, the local church administrative methods and models of operating are shifting.

Men and women of God are forming new churches that operate under a different favor in relations to the traditional democratic system.

Some are even transitions older established church into the new style of government.

Are these free of oppositions? Absolutely not! Wherever the Spirit of God is working the spirit of the Devil will try to counter it.

What must we do? "The Master's Will". His will is that we worship and praise Him and minister to the needs of His people.

Pastors and Deacons let us be about our Father's Business and not get caught up in who is in charge—that's the Holy Ghost!

If You Serve Well! You Will Be Rewarded Well!

X. Tidbits To The Deacon

1. You are selected by the congregation to assist the pastor, not pastor the pastor.

2. Never think that you have the authority to hire or fire the pastor.

3. Execute your job with humility, grace and love.

4. Never think that you cannot be removed as an active deacon of a church—you are appointed and you can be disappointed!

5. Never degrade or disrespect the pastor.

6. Never allow your disagreeing with the pastor to show in the congregation meetings or worship.

7. You have been selected to your office to help and not hurt.

8. Never allow any one in the congregation to force you into an evil plot to harm or get rid of the pastor.

9. The pastor need you to hold up his/her hands

10. When problems arise in the church, do not prejudge them too quickly—get all of the facts first!

11. Your job is vital, as it relates to the success of the local church.

12. Never show your disagreement about an issue that has been voted on in the board's meeting.

13. Always show your support to the pastor when he/she is preaching.

14. Always encourage the congregation to pray for and support the pastor.

15. You're a leader—walk in integrity and godly character.

16. Never try to belittle the pastor by trying to throw your weight (influence) around.

Remember, the church was founded without your office. By the grace of God you may one day become a pastor, and you will reap what you **"sow"**.

XI. Deacon Questionnaire:

Why is this questionnaire important? Well, it helps screen the persons who will be serving in this important and timely office.

It is my belief and conviction that before any person is selected and presented to the general church body, they should be catechized.

This process affirms orally and in writing that the person is willing to follow the principles of the Scriptures (Bible) and the guidelines of the church government.

Informing people of their responsibilities is very important. I have discovered over the years that church families and church leadership have being sub-par when it comes to making sure that the persons who serve in the office of deacon is well qualified.

I humbly beseech all Pastors and church families to rigidly catechize your Deacons as you do the Pastor. After all, they're servants and they need to be able to execute their responsibilities.

    I believe deacons should be periodic evaluate, as it relates to their performance and a regular refresher courses and seminars should be administrated to ensure that the deacons are in **tip top spiritual shape.**

    Anyone refusing to be evaluated should not be allowed to continue to serve. What a great church you will have when the pastor and the assisting deacons are all in tuned and working together. **That's Power!**

Deacon's Questionnaire Con't.

Name_____

Date_____

DOB_____

Date Joined GPMBC, Inc.

_____

Joined By: [ ] Letter   [ ] Statement
[ ]Baptism

Upon Completion return this form to:

Your Church
Street Address
City—State—Zip Code
Attn: Pastor

                         Recent Photo

Please briefly describe your salvation experience to the best of your ability.

_____
_____
_____
_____
_____
_____

1. Have you ever been ordained as a deacon?

   [] Yes   [] No

If yes, give name of church and date_____

2. Are you willing to continuously support this church
total vision and programs?
   [] Yes   [] No

3. Are you willing and able to serve as a deacon of this church?
   [] Yes   [] No

4. Have you read and understood the selection process and duties of a deacon as outlined in the in the Scriptures (Acts 6:1-7 and 1 Timothy 3.
   [] Yes   [] No

5. Have your spouse read these Scriptures too and understand them?
   [ ] Yes [ ] No

6. Are you faithful in your giving to this Church as prescribed in the bible?
   [ ] Yes [ ] No

7. Are you willing to abide by the Church's Constitution and By-Laws?
   [ ] Yes [ ] No

8. Are you willing to be faithful in your attendance to leadership and church meetings, worship services, prayer meeting and bible study?
   [ ] Yes [ ] No

9. Are you willing to accept all of your deacon's ministry assignments and with God's help and carry them out to the best of your ability?
   [ ] Yes [ ] No

10. Is your home in accordance with the Scriptures, i.e., your wife and children?
    [ ] Yes [ ] No

11. If you become disqualified from serving as a deacon in this church, will you willingly resign?
[ ] Yes   [ ] No

12. List below the areas of ministry that you believe you are gifted to serve in the life of this church i.e., worship, outreach, choir bible study.

1._____
2._____
3._____
4._____
5._____

13. Have you or your spouse ever been divorced?
[ ] Yes   [ ] No

14. What do you believe about the authority and inspiration of the Scriptures?
_____
_____
_____
_____
_____

15. In your opinion, what is the mission of the local Church.

_____
_____
_____
_____
_____
_____

16. Explain briefly who the Holy Spirit is and His purpose in the New Testament Church and the believers.

_____
_____
_____
_____
_____
_____

17. In your opinion explain how and what happens when a person is born again. Please site bible passages.

_____
_____
_____
_____

_____
_____
_____
_____

18.   Do you understand that, in this church it is not your job nor responsibility to pastor the pastor, but to support, assist, and pray for him.
    [] Yes   [] No

19.   Have you answered the above question truthfully to the best of your ability
    [] Yes   [] No

_____
Prospective Deacon: Sign

_____
Prospective Deacon Spouse: Sign

_____
Date

XII. The Author's Contact Information And Other Works

Mailing Address:
1313 Ujamaa Drive,
Raleigh, NC 27610

Phone Nos. (919) 208-0200,

Email Address:
jroger3420@aol.com

HOW TO WALK
IN YOUR DESTINY
"YOUR PATHWAY
TO VICTORY"
DR. JOSEPH R.
ROGERS, SR.

My Role In
The Local
Church
Dr. Joseph R Rogers Sr.

My Role As An Associate Minister
Servants Of God And The Senior Pastor's Armor Bearers
Dr. Joseph R. Rogers, Sr.

Christian Discipleship And The Holy Spirit
Equipping And Empowering For Kingdom Building
Dr. Joseph R Rogers Sr.

DIVORCE GOD'S WAY (FROM A BIBLICAL PERSPECTIVE)

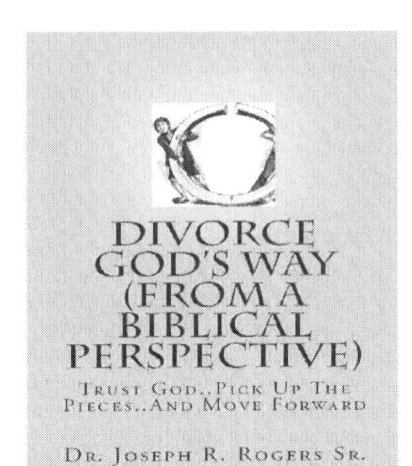

Trust God...Pick Up The Pieces...And Move Forward

Dr. Joseph R. Rogers Sr.

From The Pit To The Palace (The Ultimate VICTORY)

The African American Accomplishments And Achievements Past & Present

Dr. Joseph R. Rogers Sr.

MARRIAGE GOD'S WAY
"Keep The Fire Burning"

Dr. Joseph R. Rogers, Sr.

CHURCH LEADERSHIP
The Pastor And The Deacon

Dr. Joseph R. Rogers, Sr.

EVANGELISM 101
Tearing Down The Kingdom Of Darkness

Dr. Joseph R Rogers Sr.

Deaconesses

MY ROLE AS A DEACONESS

The Deaconess Role From A Biblical Perspective

Dr. Joseph R. Rogers Sr.

(There Is A Series of 1-39)

My Role As A Deacon

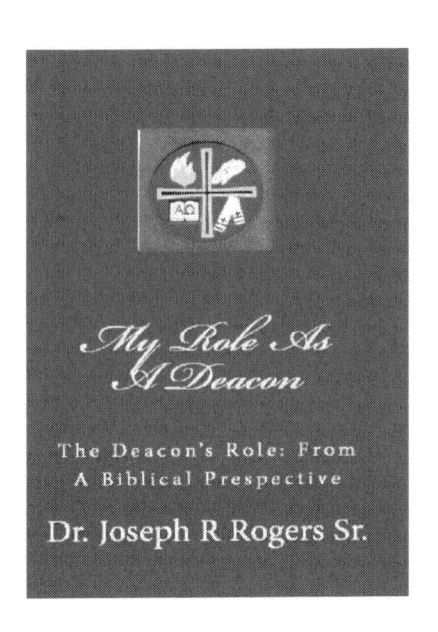

The Deacon's Role: From A Biblical Prespective

Dr. Joseph R Rogers Sr.

"WHOSO FINDETH A WIFE FINDETH A GOOD THING AND OBTAINETH FAVOR OF THE LORD." (PROVERBS 18/23)

INSIGHTS FOR CHOOSING A COMPANION

Securing The Right Companion

Dr. Joseph Roosevelt Rogers, Sr.

Men's Day Sermon Outlines 5

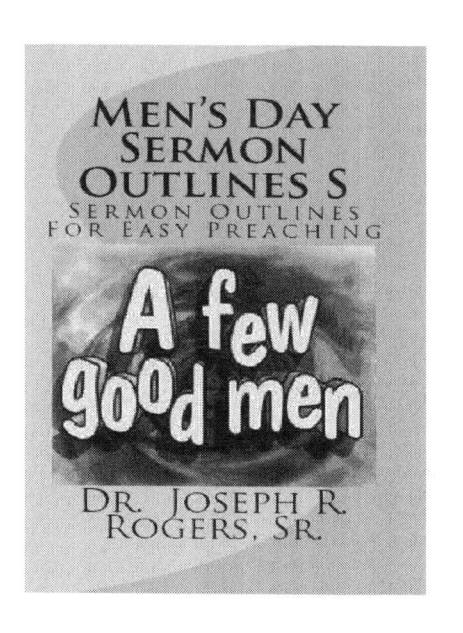

Sermon Outlines For Easy Preaching

A few good men

Dr. Joseph R. Rogers, Sr.

Blessed And Highly Favored: Physical & Spiritual Blessings

Dr. Joseph R. Rogers, Sr.

Mother's/Women's Day Sermon Series 5
Happy
Mother's
Day

MINISTERING TO THE SENIORS Dr. Joseph R. Rogers Sr.
"THE DAYS OF OUR YEARS ARE THREESCORE YEARS AND TEN; AND IF BY REASON OF STRENGTH THEY BE FOURSCORE YEARS". (PSALMS 90:10A)
Graceful Seniors
MINISTERING TO THE SENIORS
Understanding The Myths & Truths Of The Aging Process
DR. JOSEPH R. ROGERS SR.

A SERMON SERIES
ON WORSHIP (THE
POWER OF WORSHIP)
Dr. Joseph Rogers, Sr.

Church Discipline
Guidelines
Dealing With Internal
Church Discipline
Holiness
Dr. Joseph R.
Rogers Sr.

FAST
What Is Prayer/
Fasting Study Series
Dr. Joseph
Rogers, Sr.

My Role In
The Local
Church
Stay In
Your Lane
UNITY
Dr. Joseph Roosevelt
Rogers Sr.

XIII. Notes:

Note Con't.

Printed in Great Britain
by Amazon.co.uk, Ltd.,
Marston Gate.